The Rosetta Stone

Richard Parkinson

THE BRITISH MUSEUM PRESS

Copyright © 2005 The Trustees
of The British Museum

Richard Parkinson has asserted his
moral right to be identified as the
author of this work

First published in 2005 by
The British Museum Press
A division of The British Museum
Company Ltd
38 Russell Square
London WC1B 3QQ

A catalogue record for this book is
available from the British Library

ISBN-13: 978-0-7141-5021-5

ISBN-10: 0-7141-5021-5

Designed by Esterson Associates
Typeset in Miller and
Akzidenz-Grotesque
Printed and bound in China by
C&C Offset

Map by ML Design
Hieroglyphic artwork by
Richard Parkinson

Acknowledgements
It is a pleasure to thank the
following friends and colleagues:
Patricia Usick, honorary archivist
in the Department of Ancient Egypt
and Sudan, for her researches and
comments on a draft; Eric Miller
and Andrew Middleton of the
Department of Conservation and
Scientific Research; Paul Tansey
and Jon Ould of the Department
of Presentation for their displays
of the Stone; Laura Brockbank
of British Museum Press;
Mme Chateauminois; Okasha
el-Daly; Didier Devauchelle; Neil
MacGregor; Marie-Hélène Pottier,
of the Musée Champollion; Tim
Reid; Robert Simpson; Dominique
Valbelle; Simon and Elizabeth Young.

Contents

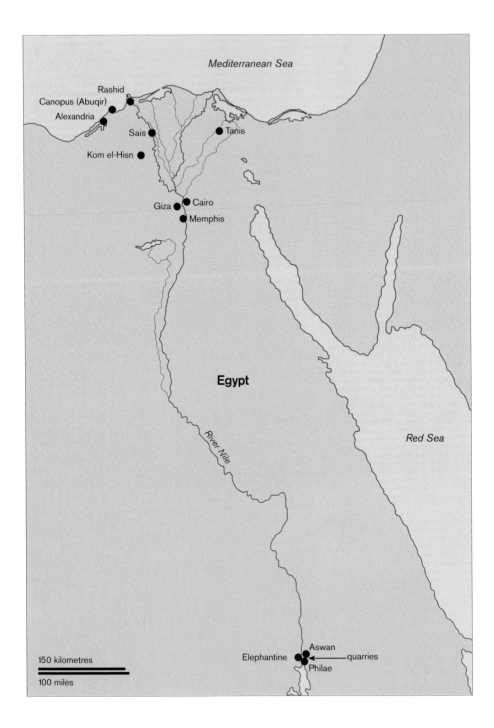

Mediterranean Sea

Rashid
Canopus (Abuqir)
Alexandria
Sais
Kom el-Hisn
Tanis

Giza ● Cairo
● Memphis

Egypt

River Nile

Red Sea

Aswan
150 kilometres   Elephantine ●──quarries
                              Philae
100 miles

Des prêtres égyptiens m'ont montré leurs antiques symboles,
signes plutôt que mots, efforts très anciens de classification
du monde et des choses, parler sépulchral d'une race morte.

Egyptian priests have shown me their antique symbols,
signs rather than words, very ancient attempts at classifying
the world and things, the sepulchral speech of a dead race.
M. Yourcenar, *Mémoires d'Hadrien* (1951)

1 The Rosetta Stone.

The 'most famous piece of rock in the world'[1]

The 'Rosetta Stone' is an irregularly shaped slab of a dark stone, 112.3 cm tall, 75.7 wide, 28.4 thick, and weighing around 762 kg (fig. 1). This fragment of an ancient stela (an inscribed slab) became the key that unlocked for Europe the mysterious hieroglyphic script of ancient Egypt. Its unique importance in our understanding of the past is due to the accidents of history over a thousand years, and it has gained its significance not from its place of manufacture, now uncertain, but from the interactions of the ancient Greek and Egyptian cultures that created it, and the modern cultures that dominated its rediscovery in 1799. This has transformed it from a broken stela into a symbol of both decipherment and also empathy across cultures and time.

The Rosetta Stone is synonymous with the Ancient Egyptian hieroglyphs that cover the statues, monuments and papyri surviving from that culture. This picture-like script was intimately bound up with Egypt's culture: it was never used elsewhere, although imitated in the kingdoms of ancient Sudan, and seems to have inspired the Proto-Sinaitic script, a possible distant ancestor of the modern alphabet. However, three other scripts and languages are found on the Rosetta Stone. The broken top is covered with 14 lines of hieroglyphs, which is less than half of the original estimated 29 lines. Below this, another Egyptian script, the cursive Demotic, occupies 32 lines, and at the bottom is an Ancient Greek text of 54 lines. Each records the text of the same decree from 196 BC. A much later stage of the Rosetta Stone's history is recorded in the English labels that were painted on the sides in the nineteenth century, when it entered the British Museum.

It is now the Museum's most visited single item, with an immense capacity to evoke wonder. The modern name 'Rosetta Stone' is, however, in many ways misleading: 'Stone' obscures its status as an ancient artefact carved in a particular culture at a particular date, and wrongly suggests that it is instead a monolithic and geological force of nature. The immediately recognizable craggy shape of the Stone is a product of chance breakages: the original edges of the stela survive along the left vertical edge, at much of the right vertical edge and along most of the bottom. The designation 'Rosetta' is also slightly misleading, since although it was discovered at the Egyptian town of Rashid, also known as Rosetta, it cannot have been originally placed there: the land on which that seaside town was built did not exist at the time of its carving, being the result of later sedimentation. Rosetta is in any case only part of the stela's 2,000-year story. Like any cultural artefact it cannot be considered in isolation: artefacts are never accidents, but are shaped by social practices and by their worlds, of which they become often the only remnants.

The creation of the Rosetta Stone

The Stone's story is fashioned by the accidents of history, involving many chance events and meetings between cultures. In 332 BC Egypt was conquered by Alexander the Great and then was ruled by a Macedonian dynasty, the Ptolemies. This dynasty, of whose monarchs Cleopatra VII (51–30 BC) was said to have been the first to learn Egyptian, ruled from the predominantly Greek city of Alexandria. Fabled as one the great cosmopolitan centres of the ancient world Alexandria has been evoked by the modern Greek poet Constantine Cavafy (1863–1933) as 'the town that teaches the world, the pinnacle of all Greece, the city most wise in all art, in every discipline of language'.[2] Greek was the official language of the court and government administration, and the dynasty saw a fusion, or juxtaposition, of cultures: this was a country in which a person who bore names in Greek and in Egyptian might live in a town with a Greek and Egyptian place-name and worship gods with Greek and Egyptian names. The Egyptian temples and their priests remained the preservers of a vibrant distinctive culture, and although they interacted with Greek literature and thinking, they were a potential source of dissident activity. The tensions between rulers and ruled seem to have centred around the temples as the strongholds of native Egyptian culture and of its formal language, but while priests were important figures in the royal administration, by the late third century BC a royal subvention financed the cost of temples, lessening their independence.

The years before the carving of the Rosetta Stone had been full of strife. The whole of the far south of Egypt was in revolt and partly controlled by rebel native kings from late in the reign of King Ptolemy IV (221–205 BC) until 186 BC. The rebellions were probably motivated by social and economic factors as well as nationalistic resentment of Greek rule. In the summer of 205 BC Ptolemy IV died suddenly in his mid-thirties, and Ptolemy V Epiphanes came to the throne in Alexandria as a six-year-old child. The accession of the new king was surrounded by courtly intrigues, which weakened the government. Ptolemy IV's death was concealed until the boy-king's mother Arsinoe had been deliberately killed in a fire, and eventually the palace was stormed by the people and soldiers, and the child pulled from his nurse to be made king: 'This was the world and he did not like it.'³ Soon afterwards in the East the Seleucid King Antiochus the Great resumed hostilities against Egypt, and these continued until 200 or 198 BC. Rebels in the Delta town of Lycopolis and in the capital Alexandria were eventually defeated in Year 8 of the reign, and they were punished as part of the coronation of the now thirteen-year-old king, apparently on 26 November 197 BC. These revolts were serious enough to disrupt the building of the great Temple of Horus at Edfu, and the new king built far fewer temples than his predecessors.

The coronation was celebrated with traditional Egyptian rites, in the traditional capital, Memphis. The High Priest of Ptah, Harmachis, son of Anemhor, crowned the child. The festival was celebrated in the presence of priestly delegates from all the areas of the country that were under allegiance to the Alexandrian court. A decree was issued in Year 9 on 27 March 196 BC to record the priests' granting of a royal cult to the king in return for his favours to them, including exemption from taxes; it is known after its place

of issue as the 'Memphis Decree'. It is one of a series of similar priestly announcements, apparently made when the priests gathered to celebrate national ceremonies in honour of the king. Although Ptolemy V was only thirteen years old when it was composed, the text describes him in traditional Egyptian terms as restoring order, 'establishing Egypt and making it perfect, his heart beneficent towards the gods', although it is also in many ways a very Greek style of document. In earlier periods the Egyptian king was the issuer of all decrees, but the Memphis Decree was issued by the indigenous priests as the creators of traditional native culture. As was always the case in Egyptian monumental texts and their idealizing vision of the world, the decree omits to mention the loss of Palestine and the revolts in the south of the country.

The substance of the decree sprung from the coexisting and competing linguistic and cultural spheres in Egypt. These also created the need to compose it three times, making it relevant to the major written cultures within the country, exemplified by the supposed users of the three scripts: the gods and priests, the Egyptian-speaking literate populace (many of whom were priests), and the Greek-speaking administration. Hieroglyphs had been used for over 3,000 years and were now understood only by specialist priests: the archaic language written in them had been dead for many centuries. It seems likely that the different versions were composed simultaneously, although the hieroglyphic version is the most artificial. In this the priests used archaistic diction, but there are also occasional 'Demoticisms' – lapses into a register closer to the language the priests usually wrote. It is probable that the Egyptian priests were sufficiently Hellenized to have drafted the decree in Greek, although the political tensions and intentions behind such a document are always hard to reconstruct.

The stone for the stela was quarried far to the south of Memphis in the rocky cataract region around Aswan – an area famous for its quarries throughout Egyptian history. The Rosetta Stone is a dark grey granite-like stone with a pink vein such as is found in the hills to the south of Aswan on the east bank of the Nile, formed some 600 million years

3 The Canopus Decree, on a stela from Kom el-Hisn in the western Nile Delta, and now in the Egyptian Museum, Cairo (220 cm high).

ago. Such hard stones were used for monumental records, statues and buildings that were intended to last for ever. It would have been roughly shaped at Aswan, transported by boat down the Nile and then carved in temple workshops in the three scripts; there are spelling mistakes in the Greek, suggesting that it was carved by specialist Egyptian temple craftsmen who were more familiar with carving the traditional Egyptian scripts. The original shape of the stela is shown in a hieroglyph that writes the word 'stela' in line 14 of the top text: ⌂. The stela would originally have had a rounded top headed by a winged sun-disk, and possibly a scene with figures in Egyptian style (fig. 2), similar to that showing the king and queen between two groups of gods on another stela with a copy of the 'Canopus Decree' that was issued in 238 BC under Ptolemy III Euergetes I (fig. 3). The stela's original height can be calculated as being around 149 cm; the sides taper slightly towards the top and are worked to an even, if unsmoothed, surface, but are not as highly finished as the front face. The texts are shallowly incised on the front surface, which is carefully polished. They are skilfully laid out, although the last two lines of the Demotic are inscribed in an expansive style to fill the space. The back face of the stela was only roughly finished, suggesting that it would have been placed upright against a wall.

The final lines of the decree describe the multi-cultural creation of the stela. The Greek version states that the decree should be inscribed on:

[a stela] of hard stone, in sacred (= hieroglyphic), and native/local (= Demotic), and Greek characters and set it up in each of the first, and second, [and third rank temples beside the image of the ever-living king].

The hieroglyphic version of this starts (right to left):

𓋴𓏏𓊃𓎡𓈖𓏤𓉐𓏤𓈖𓏪 ...

and reads:

on a stela of hard stone in the script of god's words (= hieroglyphic script), the script of documents (= Demotic script), and the letters of the Aegeans (= Greek) and set it up in all the temples of first, second, and third rank, beside the statue of the Dual King Ptolemy living forever, beloved of Ptah, the God who Appears (= Greek epithet 'Epiphanes'), Lord of Goodness.

It is uncertain how literally the instruction to set up the decree in all the temples is to be understood. Other copies of the decree are known from Elephantine in the south and sites in the Delta, but it is probable that the cult was not established in all Egyptian temples as simultaneously as the decree implies: texts and historical reality never quite coincide. The stela was probably erected at a more ancient site than Rashid, further inland: the Egyptologist Labib Habachi has suggested the royal city of Sais (modern Sa el-Hagar), nearby on the same branch of the Nile (fig. 4). Sais was famous in Classical accounts for its great stone temple and secret priestly wisdom, and was described by Herodotus in the fifth century BC, with its magnificent temple to the goddess Neith, royal tombs, obelisks, statues and the sacred lake. Today, as with so many Delta sites, little survives of the town or temple; the denuded site is currently being studied by the Egypt Exploration Society and University of Durham Mission to Sa el-Hagar in collaboration with the Supreme Council of Antiquities.

It is also uncertain exactly where in the temple the stela would have been erected. The text states that it was to be placed 'beside the statue of the Dual King Ptolemy', which was the object of worship. The decree describes a cult-image of the king which is to be placed in a shrine in each temple sanctuary, but the stela was to be placed outside, next to another statue 'in the manner of Egyptian work' of the king that was to be erected 'in the public part of the temple'. The text on the front of the stela would have been clearly legible if placed outside in the sunlight. From surviving traces it seems possible that the signs were originally filled with a light red pigment. As already mentioned, the rough back

5 A granite stela of Ptolemy VI Philometor standing against the second pylon of the Temple of Isis on the sacred island of Philae.

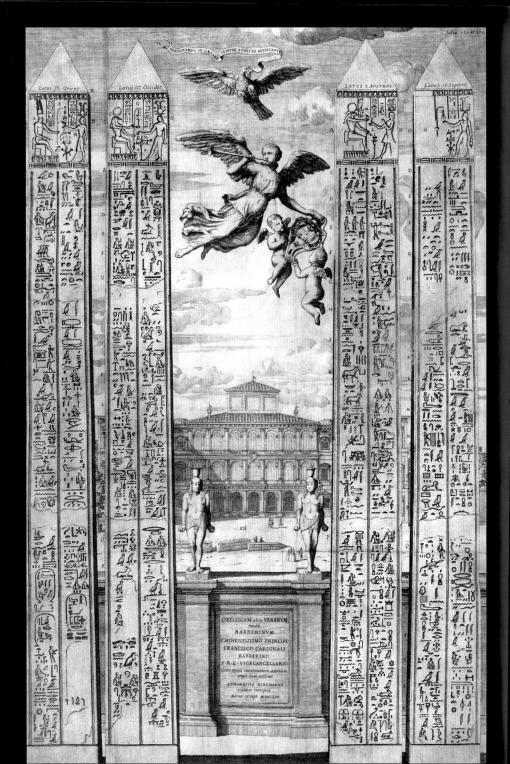

6 The last Egyptian
obelisk commissioned
by the emperor Hadrian
in AD 130, as copied
by Athanasius Kircher
in 1652–4 (*Oedipus
Aegyptiacus* III, 270).

surface of the Stone shows that it was placed up against a wall, and this was probably in the outer area of a temple, rather as a stela of Year 24 of Ptolemy VI Philometor (ruled 180–145 BC) on the sacred island of Philae, which is placed against the outer face of the second pylon of the Temple of Isis (fig. 5). This stela is in the outer reaches of a sacred enclosure of restricted access, not within the main temple building, so that it was on display to a (probably select) public. How many of these could have read it is uncertain, and such hieroglyphic texts were addressed to the gods more than to the passing populace. The Rosetta Stone probably stood in the temple precincts of Sais for several centuries.

The loss of hieroglyphs

The Ptolemaic dynasty came to an end with the famous suicide of Cleopatra VII in 30 BC, and Egypt became part of the Roman Empire. Roman emperors of the first two centuries AD still commissioned hieroglyphic inscriptions, not only in the Egyptian heartland, but also on obelisks to be erected in Italy, such as that of Hadrian in memory of his lover Antinous, who drowned in the Nile in AD 130 (fig. 6). This was probably placed in a mortuary chapel at Rome, or at the Villa Adriana near Tivoli, which was later the source of many Egyptian works for Renaissance excavators. It now stands in the gardens of the Monte Pincio, Rome, erected there in 1822, the year that the hieroglyphic script began to be deciphered. The inscription on the sides of the obelisk is skilfully composed in classical Ancient Egyptian, and possibly by a lector-priest of the temple at Akhmim called Petehornebkhem, who is known from a funerary stela, although the inscription was probably carved onto the obelisk in Italy. The hieroglyphic script was by now a sacred system whose use was increasingly restricted to temples and similar monuments, cut off from the living scripts and languages of Egypt; its last flowering on temple walls was in the third century AD.

As Egypt became Christian following the conversion of Emperor Constantine the temples gradually closed, and the Byzantine emperor Theodosius issued a decisive edict shutting them in AD 392. The temple at Sais would have

7 The latest known
hieroglyphic inscription,
carved by a priest on
24 August AD 394 in the
Gate of Hadrian on the
island of Philae. The
Demotic inscription is
in front of the god's legs.

been closed at this time. The latest known hieroglyphic inscription, however, is found on the island of Philae, carved next to a relief of the Nubian god Mandulis that was added to a temple gateway erected earlier by Hadrian (AD 117–38), leading towards the supposed tomb of Osiris (the Abaton) on the nearby island of Biga (fig. 7). It reads (right to left):

> Before Mandulis son of Horus, by the hand of Nesmeterakhem, son of Nesmeter, the Second Priest of Isis, for all time and eternity. Words spoken by Mandulis, Lord of the Abaton, great god.

A Demotic inscription below it reads:

> I, Nesmeterakhem, the scribe of the House of Writings [?] of Isis, son of Nesmeterpanakhet the Second Priest of Isis, and his mother Eseweret, I performed work on this figure of Mandulis for all time, because he is fair of face towards me. Today, the Birthday of Osiris, his dedication feast, year 110.

The inscription, in the same two Egyptian scripts found on the Rosetta Stone, is dated by counting from the accession of Emperor Diocletian in AD 285 and corresponds to 24 August 394. With this specialist priest the hieroglyphic script disappears. The figure and inscription were carved in connection with the visits of the pagan Blemmye tribe from the Red Sea hills to the south-east in order to pay homage to the goddess Isis. These visits forced the Byzantine emperors to allow the temple to remain open despite the Christianization of Egypt and the earlier edict of Theodosius. In the fifth century AD Demotic was still occasionally written in the temple, and it is uncertain exactly when the last person to use, or at least read, the ancient scripts would have lived. There were by now Christian churches on the island, and the final centuries of pagan Philae passed into Christian legend. A later Coptic history of the first monk-bishops of Philae tells how Bishop Apa Macedonius once deviously gained access to a sacred falcon in the temple and burned it. Between AD 535 and 537 the emperor Justinian ordered the temple's closure, the imprisonment of the priests and the removal of its statues to Constantinople. The temple was rededicated to Saint Stephen, further churches were erected on the sacred island and the figure of the god carved by Nesmeterakhem was defaced. The hieroglyphic and Demotic scripts did not die because other more efficient scripts evolved, but because of political factors. Although scripts can appear to be abstract systems, they are bound by culture and time and cannot be separated from the institutions that create and use them.

The fate of the Rosetta Stone at this period is unknown. As the temples were closed, they were often quarried and their stone reused, and in the flat agricultural land of the Delta statues and blocks of hard stone have been moved between sites throughout Egyptian history. At some point the stela must have been toppled and smashed into its present shape, breaking along the line of the vein of pink granite. It may have lain on its front face, given the lack of erosion and damage there. It was eventually moved to Rashid, where it was used in the construction of a fortress by the Mamluk ruler of Egypt, Sultan Qaitbay (AD 1468–95), in order to defend this important port on the branch of the Nile. All modern attempts to find further fragments of the stela at Rashid have failed; it was probably already broken when it was moved there, unless there are further fragments concealed inside the walls of the fortress (other fragments of monuments from Sais are still visible built into its walls). Without the building activity of Qaitbay the stela might never have survived.

It is possible that some knowledge of the hieroglyphic script survived in Egypt after the closure of the temples, but it was actively attacked by Coptic monks such as Apa Shenute (died AD 466), who denounced its idolatrous appearance as 'prescriptions for murdering man's soul … written in blood' that portray nonsensical 'likenesses of snakes and scorpions, the dogs and cats, the crocodiles and frogs, the foxes, the other reptiles …'.[4] Later, medieval Arab scholars showed great interest in ancient Egyptian culture, visiting temples, copying inscriptions and describing scenes on temple walls that filled the visitor 'with wonder and amazement'.[5] One scholar, Ahmad bin Abu Bakr ibn Wahshiyah, who stayed in Egypt in the ninth to tenth centuries, wrote a treatise on scripts in which he not only interpreted hieroglyphs as pictorial images, but also provided an alphabet in which hieroglyphs represented single letters (albeit only occasionally correctly).

However, it was always the pictorial appearance of hieroglyphs that struck visitors, including the Greeks and Romans, who assumed that they were symbolic pictures and not a script. In fact the hieroglyphic script is a mixture of sound- and picture-signs recording the Egyptian language. For example, the word for 'cat' is written: 𓏏𓏭𓃠. The first, two-letter, sign writes *mi* 𓏇, a second sign complements this, writing the letter *i* 𓏭 a second time, and a third sign provides the next consonant *w* 𓅱. The final sign, as in most words, is a 'determinative', a picture-sign expressing the lexical class of the word, here showing that the word refers to a feline 𓃠. The phonetic reality behind the signs is difficult to reconstruct, since the script did not write full vowels, and the sounds would have changed although the written form of the word remained largely unchanged for a few thousand years. Egyptologists transcribe the word for cat as *miw*, and a conventional pronunciation is *miu*, but the word may have sounded something like *emou*.

The Greeks' interpretation of the script as a set of symbolic pictures recording concepts without the use of language was not due to simple misunderstanding. It was in part a direct result of the Egyptians' tendency, particularly in the Graeco-Roman period, to foreground the script's pictorial nature by using wordplay to allow sound-signs to take on a shape appropriate for the word's meaning. This tendency is extreme in a hymn to the ram-god Khnum carved in the Temple of Esna in the late first century AD, where almost every sign becomes a picture of a ram (see left), and ironically only the opening words can now be read with any certainty. This system, with its elaboration on the script's symbolic aspects, is a final flowering of intellectual sophistication that ensured the tradition's survival by captivating the imagination of future generations.

8 An obelisk of King
Apries (589–570 BC),
erected on an
allegorical elephant
designed by Bernini in
1667 outside the church
of Santa Maria sopra
Minerva in Rome.

As the centuries following the Christianization of Egypt passed, all knowledge of the realities of the hieroglyphic script was lost to European scholars, and hieroglyphs became associated with anything antique and exotic. This was partly due to Egyptian culture's distinctive religious and funerary practices, but the hostile images of Egypt in the Bible compounded the indecipherable repute of hieroglyphs as unholy mysteries. In an age where travel to Egypt was difficult few Egyptian monuments could be studied by European scholars apart from those moved to Italy by the Roman emperors. Accounts of hieroglyphs by Classical authors survived into the European Renaissance, but they conveyed little understanding of how hieroglyphs were read linguistically, and the Renaissance tradition continued to present each sign as a symbol. This view of hieroglyphs can be seen in an obelisk of King Apries (589–570 BC), which was erected on an allegorical base by the artist Gianlorenzo Bernini in 1667 outside the church of Santa Maria sopra Minerva in Rome (fig. 8). The whole is an emblem of strength of mind (the elephant) supporting wisdom (the hieroglyphic obelisk). Bernini's contemporary, the Jesuit antiquarian Athanasius Kircher (1602–80), produced bizarre decodings of inscriptions as highly symbolic mystic pronouncements. For example, he read the name 'Antinous' on Hadrian's obelisk as an elaborate statement about the nature and powers of 'the tutelary spirit of the clouds' (see fig. 6). However, his work stimulated interest in Egyptian matters and also in Coptic, the language of Christian Egypt and now known to be the descendent of the language of pharaonic Egypt. For these pioneers, it was impossible to distinguish accurate and inaccurate information in the earlier accounts. The potentially fruitful insights of the early Arab scholars remained unused by the Europeans, although the treatise of Ahmad bin Abu Bakr ibn Wahshiyah was known to Kircher, and an English translation was published in 1806 as *Ancient Alphabets and Hieroglyphic Characters Explained, with an Account of the Egyptian Priests*. This was based on a manuscript recently acquired in Cairo, where, as the translator Joseph Hammer noted, 'it had escaped the researchers of the French *savans* [scholars]'.

The rediscovery of the Stone

By the eighteenth century the 'mysteries' encoded by the hieroglyphs were exercising the scholars of the European Enlightenment. Scientific studies of ancient scripts and languages were becoming more numerous, including the comparative work on Sanskrit by Sir William Jones (1746–94). In the 1760s Abbé Jean-Jaques Barthélemy (1716–95), who deciphered the Phoenician script on the basis of bilingual coin legends, suggested that the oval rings ('cartouches') in Egyptian inscriptions might contain royal names, many of which were known from Classical authors. The great impediments to progress with Egyptian hieroglyphs were the lack of a large corpus of accurately copied inscriptions, the lack of any bilingual inscriptions and the false assumption that the script was not based on language, compounded by ignorance of the language of pharaonic Egypt.

The Egyptian campaign of Napoleon of 1798–1801 was in many ways a turning point in the modern European history of ancient Egypt. The campaign had political and colonial aims against Ottoman rule in Egypt, and against the English Empire, but it also had symbolic orientalist overtones, since it colonized, in the name of the Enlightenment, a country that was supposedly the origin of all wisdom. The French justified this imperial enterprise by claiming that it would rescue the ancient country from a supposed state of modern barbarism, but the Egyptian historian Abd al-Rahman al-Jabarti (1754–1822) saw the start of the occupation in July 1798 from a very different perspective as 'the beginning of a period marked by great battles ... miseries multiplied without end'. The invading force was accompanied by a body of scientists, scholars and artists, initially numbering 151 persons (fig. 9). Their work culminated in the magnificent *Description de l'Égypte*, whose volumes included antiquities, the modern state of the country and its natural history, and which were published in the years after the French withdrawal (between 1809 and 1828). Although it provided access to many more inscriptions than had been previously available to European scholars, its attempts to analyse its discoveries

were hampered by the French scholars' inability to read hieroglyphs or to copy them accurately, which caused great confusion about the relative chronology of the monuments they published. The image of Egypt presented in the text volumes drew on Classical traditions, and was dominated by European ideas of Egyptian religion as a cult of nature, and of its priests as seekers after scientific truth rather than theologians. One visual consequence of the publication was the unleashing of a tide of exotic Egyptomania in European art and design.

The discovery of the Rosetta Stone seems to have been made in mid-July 1799, shortly before the land battle of Abuqir on 25 July. Even in the middle of the fighting it was quickly recognized as 'a most valuable relic of antiquity, the feeble but only yet discovered link of the Egyptian to the known languages'.[6] Published accounts of its early history vary in details, but we do know that it was discovered on the west bank of the Nile, at the prosperous coastal town of Rashid. The French were preparing fortifications there against an imminent attack from the English and Ottoman forces who had landed at Abuqir on 14 July, in the ruined fortress of Qaitbay, now renamed by the French Fort Julien (fig. 10). The exact spot of the discovery was apparently inside the outer wall, under what is now an internal turret.

The Stone was found during work that was being conducted by a twenty-three-year-old officer of the Engineers, recently arrived at Rashid, Pierre François Xavier Bouchard (1771–1822), who was working under Citizen d'Hautpol, the head of the Engineering Battalion. Bouchard immediately realized that it was part of a stela inscribed in three scripts. Of these, the incomplete hieroglyphic section and the Greek section were easily recognizable, but the middle section, in the script now known as Demotic, was initially assumed to be Syriac. Bouchard reported the find to the French general, Abdallah-Jacques Menou (1750–1810), who was then in Rosetta. The general had the Stone taken to his tent and cleaned, and he also arranged for a translation of the Greek to be made, which confirmed that the inscriptions recorded the same text in three different scripts. Attempts to locate any additional fragments of the Stone – 'worth their weight in diamonds'[7] – in the vicinity were unsuccessful, although they were undertaken immediately and over several subsequent years (later, in 1818, Thomas Young would note in a letter that 'Mr Salt [the British pro-consul in Egypt] was empowered by the British government to expend a liberal sum in digging in the neighbourhood of Fort St Julien, or otherwise, in pursuit of this object').

News of the discovery spread quickly. A letter from the engineer Michel-Ange Lancret (1774–1807) was received

10 The interior of Fort Julien, the site of the discovery of the Rosetta Stone, showing an inscribed block built into the walls.

by scholars at the Institut d'Egypte (Egyptian Institute), founded by Napoleon in Cairo, at its meeting of 29 July, together with news of a French victory at Abuqir. The Stone itself reached Cairo under the charge of Bouchard in mid-August, as Napoleon was departing. It was deposited at the Institute, which was housed in the requisitioned palace of Hassan Khashef (off the modern Sharia el-Nasriyya, north of the Saiyida Zeinab mosque), and 'at this news, each man ran to see the marvellous stone'.[8] The discovery of what might be the 'key' to hieroglyphs was publicly announced in the *Courier* (sic) *de l'Égypte* on 15 September (no. 37). However, it proved difficult to copy the Stone's inscriptions by hand. The expedition's senior orientalist, Jean-Joseph Marcel, identified the middle section as Demotic, an Egyptian script known from Classical authors, and with Nicolas-Jacques Conté he realized that the stone could be used as a printing block to produce copies of the texts. By the autumn of 1800 these had reached Paris; it was copies such as these that would eventually enable the decipherment of the script, rather than the Stone itself.

27

The year 1801 saw the progressive surrender of the French to the British and Ottoman forces, which included forces from British India. General Menou was to hold out in Alexandria until August, determined to maintain the French occupation at all costs. The British landed at Abuqir bay in March, and the bloody battle of Canopus followed. The Institute left Cairo for Alexandria in early April, transporting the Stone with them; this ironically delayed the Stone's departure from Egypt, since, despite Menou's orders to fight to the death, the French withdrew from Cairo. Under the terms of this capitulation they returned to France with their equipment intact in July 1801, and if the Stone had remained in Cairo it too would probably have left for France before the final defeat. As it was, the Stone remained in Alexandria with the French scholars and Menou, whose relationship with them was increasingly fraught. He refused to acknowledge the surrender of Cairo but was finally forced to concede on 26 August.

The 'Capitulation of Alexandria' was signed on 31 August by Captain Pasha Hussein, representing the Ottoman rulers of Egypt, the British General John H. Hutchinson (1757–1832), the British Admiral George Keith (1746–1823) and the French General Menou. Article 16 was contested by Menou, but as signed it insisted that the French scholars should surrender everything that they had acquired in Egypt 'as public property' to the British general, although they could keep the scientific instruments they had brought from France. The 'public property' included the Rosetta Stone and their collection of some twenty-five other stone antiquities. After Menou had signed the capitulation the French scholars were horrified to learn that they were to give up both the collections and their records for the planned *Description*. They made an impassioned plea to Hutchinson through the diplomat and antiquary William Hamilton (1777–1859), who was in Egypt to oversee the French evacuation, and this secured the agreement that their notes and natural history collections could be construed as personal property and kept by them.

Meanwhile Menou was trying in various ways to retain the Stone for France by arguing that the antiquities were also personal property, and in particular that the Stone was his. Hutchinson, however, was determined to secure the Stone and repeatedly denied any claims in a fortnight-long exchange of letters. As Menou eventually remarked: 'You want it, Monsieur le Général, and you shall have it because you are the stronger.'[9] The accounts later published by various English participants in this drama differ in details. The negotiations over the surrender of the antiquities in September included the Reverend (later Professor) Edward Daniel Clarke (1769–1822), who later recalled:

> We remained near the outside of the tent; and soon heard the French General's voice elevated as usual, and in strong terms of indignation remonstrating against the injustice of the demands made upon him. The words *'Jamais on n'a pillé le monde!'* ['Never has the world been so pillaged!'] diverted us highly, as coming from a leader of plunder and devastation....[10]

A Colonel Turner (1766–1843) later asserted that when the French army learned of the English plan to possess the antiquities, they tore off the packing and protection that had been put round the Stone for its transport, and that 'it was thrown upon its face'.[11] It is impossible to tell how far these accounts are reliable and how far shaped by nationalist sympathies and personal concerns. According to Clarke's account, a French officer and a member of the Institute eventually took the Stone from where it had been hidden under mats in a warehouse with Menou's other baggage and handed it over to Hamilton, Clarke and a Mr Cripps in an Alexandrian street, after which, on the French officer's advice, it was hastily transferred to a 'place of safety'. Turner, however, later described how he had 'carried off the stone, without any injury, but with some difficulty, from the narrow streets to my house, amid the sarcasm of numbers of French officers and men'. Despite all this the French scholars were later allowed to take a cast of the Stone before they left Egypt at the end of September. The English themselves withdrew in 1803, paving the way for the rule of Mohammed Ali (reigned 1805–49), who in 1835

11 The nineteenth-century painted texts on the sides of the Rosetta Stone.

issued a decree banning the export of antiquities and making an initial attempt to protect the country's pharaonic heritage from plunder and destruction.

Late in 1801 Turner embarked on the HMS *L'Égyptienne* and set sail for England with the Rosetta Stone, which he called a 'proud trophy of the arms of Britain – not plundered from defenceless inhabitants, but honourably acquired by the fortune of war'. Most of the other antiquities travelled on another ship. News of the Stone had first reached England in the *Gentleman's Magazine* for 1801, and the ship arrived at Portsmouth in February 1802. The Stone was placed in the Society of Antiquaries, London, on 11 March, and the Society decided in July to have plaster casts taken. These were sent to the universities of Oxford, Cambridge, Edinburgh and Dublin. Others were made for the French to collate for the illustration in the *Description de l'Égypte*; the Stone eventually appeared as plates 52–4 in volume V of the Antiquities section (1822), extra copies of which were made. Full-sized engravings were also issued by the Society of Antiquaries in 1802–3, and these engravings of 'this precious monument' were widely distributed throughout Europe and America, to universities and learned institutions.

The Stone itself was officially donated to the British Museum by George III, and in June 1802 it entered the Museum's buildings in Bloomsbury, together with the other antiquities taken from the French expedition. This group included the sarcophagus of King Nectanebo II (EA 10), a colossal granite fist (EA 9; see fig. 9) and a statue of a high

priest of Amun named Roy (EA 81). These were to 'be seen
in the outer court of that building. Many of them were so
extremely massive, that it was found necessary to make
wooden frames for them'.[12] The Rosetta Stone still bears
nationalistic texts painted on the sides (fig. 11):

CAPTURED IN EGYPT BY THE BRITISH ARMY IN 1801

on the left edge of the slab, and on the right:

PRESENTED BY KING GEORGE III

The arrival of these monuments made the Museum
realize that its then home, the seventeenth-century
Montagu House, was inadequate (they were too heavy for
the floors). A new range of rooms, known as the Townley
Gallery, was added to the mansion in 1808 to hold Egyptian
and Classical sculptures (the 'Townley marbles'); the
Rosetta Stone moved from the wooden shelters in the court
into the main hall of the gallery. Montagu House and its
extension were eventually replaced by the present neo-
classical buildings designed by Robert Smirke (1781–1867),
and in 1834 the Stone was moved into the sculpture gallery,
where it still rests. In the mid-nineteenth century it was
given the inventory number that it still bears: EA
(= Egyptian Antiquities) 24. For many years the Stone was
displayed at a semi-horizontal angle, mounted in an iron
cradle (fig. 12). Small rectangular areas on the sides of the
Stone were carved away so that the arms of the cradle would

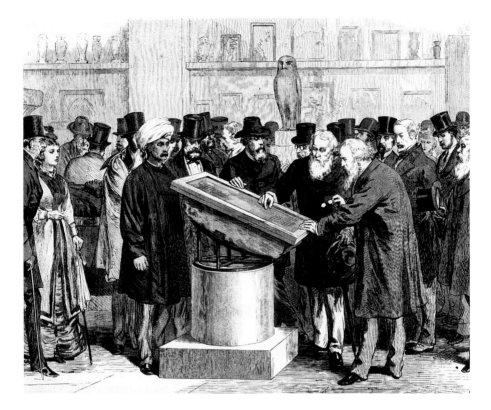

hold it firmly; and two crossed lines were incised in the
middle of the back face to help centre it in the cradle.
The Stone was initially displayed without any cover, and
instructions were given to the Museum attendants to be
particularly watchful that no one should touch it. In 1847
the Trustees reluctantly agreed that the Stone should be
covered with a glazed frame. The incised signs were filled
with white chalk early in its museum history, a procedure
that was designed to make the text more legible, and
carnauba wax was applied to the surface to help protect it.
The inscribed stela was made to look like a piece of black-
and-white printed text laid out on an angled reading desk,
as if silently ignoring its existence as an ancient monument
and subsuming it into the world of Western printing, and
this display remained much the same for almost two
centuries (see fig. 20).

The decipherment of ancient Egypt

While the Stone stood in Montagu House and in the Townley Gallery renewed European attempts to decipher Egyptian hieroglyphs whirled around it. The Demotic script on the Stone, which was more complete than the hieroglyphic section, played an immense part because scholars attempting to 'decode' it were not misled by assumptions that it was a symbolic system. The French orientalist, Baron Silvestre de Sacy (1758–1838), achieved the first breakthrough with the Demotic, identifying personal names, including that of Ptolemy, but he was incorrect in his analysis of the individual signs. In 1802 the Swedish diplomat J.H. Åkerblad (1763–1819) published his identification of several important features of the Demotic, including the third person pronouns, and correlated them with their Coptic equivalents, as well as isolating the Demotic equivalents of 'Egypt', 'the temples', 'many', 'the king', and 'Greek'. However, his discoveries about the Demotic did not challenge the false premises about the hieroglyphic script.

The two main protagonists in the mythology that has arisen around the European decipherment of the hieroglyphic script were Thomas Young (1773–1829) and Jean-François Champollion (1790–1832). Champollion was born at Figeac in Quercy on 23 December 1790 (fig. 13). He was a highly precocious, brilliantly imaginative scholar and linguist. His fascination with Egypt began at an early age: Baron Jean Baptiste Joseph Fourier (1768–1830), who had worked on the *Description* and had been perpetual secretary of the Cairo Institute, was appointed to be prefect of Isère when he returned to France in 1801; it is said that he told tales of Egypt to the ten-year-old. A copy of the *Courier* report of the Stone's discovery reached Champollion's elder brother and life-long mentor, Jacques-Joseph (1778–1867), in 1802, and the elder Champollion presented a paper on the Rosetta Stone that year to the Société des Sciences et Arts de Grenoble. He advised Jean-François that if he was interested in hieroglyphs, he should study the inscription. At the age of sixteen the younger Champollion presented a paper to the Grenoble Académie arguing that Coptic was

13 Jean-François
Champollion holding
his hieroglyphic
'alphabet', a portrait
attributed to Mme
de Rumilly, c. 1823.

the language of ancient Egypt, a belief that, although not
original, laid the foundation of his later achievements. In
1807 the two brothers left for Paris; the younger studied
under Silvestre de Sacy for Arabic, and acquired a full
familiarity with all the languages that were then considered
relevant to Egyptian, including Sanskrit and Chinese. He
was also taught Coptic by a Coptic priest. Before he was
nineteen he had been awarded a chair at the University of
Grenoble together with his brother, and Napoleon himself
signed the necessary paper making him a Doctor in 1809.

   In 1814 Champollion wrote to the Royal Society, whose
Foreign Secretary was Young, starting a correspondence
that continued until Young's death. He wrote that he had

only an engraving of the Stone made by the English Royal Society and the French copy in the *Description*, and since these differed in some respects, he requested a cast. Difficulties over the accuracy of copies of inscriptions were a persistent problem, and epigraphy was a potential object of nationalistic competition.

Thomas 'Phenomenon' Young was a distinguished and internationally acknowledged polymathic genius, now principally remembered for his work on physiological optics and the theory of light; he was also a pioneer of the light bulb (later perfected by Thomas Edison) (fig. 14). Young obliged only by checking the passages Champollion requested. He himself had recently become interested in

the Rosetta Stone through a papyrus belonging to a friend, Sir W. Rouse Boughton, and he worked on the Egyptian script during summer vacations at Worthing on the south coast of England in 1814–18. By 1816 Young could identify the name Ptolemy as a cartouche on the hieroglyphic section of the Stone (⟨𝖓𝖚⟩), and with the help of the Demotic versions he assigned the correct values of *p, t, ma/m, i, s* to five signs, as well as incorrect values to a further eight (see left for the cartouche transcribed correctly).

To reconcile this analysis with the Classical accounts of hieroglyphs, he proposed that only foreign names such as Ptolemy were written alphabetically, and that other words were written symbolically. Young suggested that Demotic and hieroglyphic signs were related by shape. By systematically comparing lines of the text between three scripts, he succeeded in correlating words such as 'king', 'and', and 'Egypt'. He isolated many Demotic word groups successfully, but he was unable reliably to produce analyses of them. Nevertheless, he could identify quite a remarkable number of hieroglyphic word groups using copies of other inscriptions, and he could suggest their meanings correctly, as summarized in a letter written in 1818 for the British dilettante, antiquarian and traveller William John Bankes (1786–1855) (fig. 15). Although he realized that Demotic was not a purely alphabetic script and that it included ideograms as well as phonetic signs, he failed to apply this insight to hieroglyphs. He resolutely maintained that hieroglyphs were symbolic and that the phonetic signs were used only 'in some particular cases, and not universally employed where sounds were required'.[13]

Bankes travelled in Egypt and the Near East between 1815 and 1819, and at Young's request he copied many inscriptions. In 1815 he came upon an obelisk at Philae and had the monument brought to England, where it finally arrived in 1821 (after passing through the port of Rashid en route). The obelisk is inscribed with hieroglyphs, but on the base Greek inscriptions record official correspondence between Ptolemy VIII Euergertes II and the priests of Isis on Philae in 124 BC concerning tax exemption. Bankes, Young and the English collector and pro-consul in Egypt,

15 A letter written by Thomas Young to William Bankes' father in 1817 listing the main hieroglyphic groups known to him at this date.

Henry Salt (1780–1827), considered that the hieroglyphs and Greek must represent the same text, thus providing another potential bilingual key. In this they were mistaken, as Champollion recognized, but Bankes correctly supposed that a cartouche on the obelisk should write the name of Cleopatra III, the queen of Ptolemy VIII, who was mentioned in the Greek, although he was unable to read the individual signs. This identification remained unpublished, although Young adopted and used it. In 1821 Bankes issued a publication of the obelisk, and in some copies he added in pencil the name 'Cleopatra' beside the relevant cartouche. The presumed bilingual nature of the inscriptions generated a brief period of fame for the obelisk as a second

16 The Philae obelisk standing outside the house of William Bankes at Kingston Lacy, Dorset.

'Rosetta Stone'. It was only erected in 1839, and two years later Bankes was forced to flee England after being committed for trial (for having sex with a soldier in Green Park, London). The obelisk still stands in the grounds of Kingston Lacy, among the swallows and cedars, overlooked by the roughly contemporaneous Iron-Age hill fort of Badbury Rings (fig. 16).

In France Champollion's political sympathies for Napoleon had caused him to be deprived of his post in Grenoble, and he arrived in Paris in July 1821 to live with his brother, then secretary to Baron Bon-Joseph Dacier (1742–1833), who was perpetual secretary of the Académie des Inscriptions et Belles Lettres in Paris. In December 1821 he compared the number of signs on the Rosetta Stone with the number of Greek words (1,419 and 486 respectively), and showed that the script could not be purely logographic, with a single picture representing each word, but he still believed that the signs were 'things and not sounds'.

By this date Young had proposed a set of alphabetic signs used to write the names of Ptolemy and Cleopatra, publishing these findings in the *Supplement to the Encyclopedia Britannica* (4th edition) in 1819. A copy of the inscriptions on the Bankes obelisk reached Champollion in 1822 and he arrived at the same conclusion as Young about the alphabetic signs in the names Ptolemy and Cleopatra. From these names he had fourteen alphabetic signs, which were sufficient for him to decipher the cartouches of other members of the Ptolemaic Dynasty and of the Roman emperors, expanding the alphabet as he progressed. It was later claimed by the English that Champollion's work was based, without acknowledgement, on Young's published work, and also on Bankes' theory about the name on the obelisk.

Champollion's brilliant insight about the true nature of the hieroglyphic script is often presented as an almost mythical event, as a moment of superhuman revelation, as follows: on 14 September 1822, in the rue Mazarine, Paris, he received copies of inscriptions from the great rock-cut temple of Rameses II at Abu Simbel and other sites. These had been sent by a travelling friend, the architect of the Arc de Triomphe, Jean Nicolas Huyot (1780–1840), who had made the drawings while he was at the site with Bankes' party in 1819 (fig. 17). A drawing from Abu Simbel included the cartouche with the signs ⚬̇. Champollion could read the final two signs ⚍ as *ss*, and his knowledge of Coptic suggested that the sun-shaped sign ⚬ might represent the word for sun, in Coptic *re*; hence the name could be read as *Re?ses*, instantly suggesting the royal name familiar from the accounts of the Greek historian Manetho (third century BC) as *Ramesses*. The reading of 𓅓 as *m* was provided by a group of signs on the Rosetta Stone which could be matched with the Greek word for 'birthday', in Coptic *houms*. Champollion's reading of the cartouche was correct, although he believed that each sound-sign represented one consonant (taking 𓅓 as *m*), whereas some signs were subsequently recognized as representing more than one (𓅓 actually being *ms*).

This reading was corroborated by another cartouche 𓅝 which had an ibis 𓅝, the bird sacred to the god Thoth, instead of the sun-disk. Young had guessed that this might

Ramesses

Touthmosis

Pl. IV.

Tableau des Signes Phonétiques
des Écritures hiéroglyphique et Démotique des anciens Égyptiens

Lettres Grecques	Signes Démotiques	Signes Hiéroglyphiques
A		
B		
Γ		
Δ		
E		
Z		
H		
Θ		
I		
K		
Λ		
M		
N		
Ξ		
O		
Π		
P		
Σ		
T		
Υ		
Φ		
Ψ		
X		
Ꙋ		
ΤΟ. Τα.		

18 Champollion's chart of Demotic and hieroglyphic alphabetic signs with their Greek equivalents from his *Lettre à M. Dacier*, 1822.

be another name preserved by the Greek historians as *Touthmosis*, but now Champollion could read it sign by sign as Thothmes or Tuthmes. From these names Champollion realized that the script included mostly sound-signs but also picture-signs writing words. More importantly he realized that it was used to write native names from the pharaonic period and so could have been used to write the Egyptian language in the same manner. According to the account of his nephew, Aimé Champollion-Figeac, he rushed to his brother's room in the Institute on the afternoon of the same day, cried 'I've done it' ('Je tiens mon affaire!') and collapsed in a dead faint lasting five days.

Champollion's famous report, the *Lettre à M. Dacier* (Letter to M. Dacier), was read at the Académie des Inscriptions et Belles Lettres in Paris on Friday 27 September 1822, a romantically dark and rainy day, in a romantically eventful year that saw the Declaration of Independence in Greece (from the Ottoman Empire). Bankes' friend Lord Byron was writing *Don Juan* and the plans for the present buildings of the British Museum were being drawn up by Robert Smirke. The *Lettre* is addressed to Bon-Joseph Dacier, the Academy's perpetual secretary, and was officially dated 22 September to match the day on which its text was completed (fig. 18). In this report Champollion described the alphabet that was used to write non-Egyptian names, and in the concluding pages he tentatively announced that he was certain that the phonetic signs were an integral part of earlier 'pure hieroglyphic writing'. Among the select audience was the great Prussian natural scientist and explorer Alexander von Humboldt (1769–1859), and also Thomas Young, whose initial reaction is recorded in a letter written to Sir William Hamilton on the Sunday after the reading:

I have found here, or rather recovered, Mr. Champollion, junior, who has been living for these ten years on the Inscription of Rosetta, and who has lately been making some steps in Egyptian literature, which really appear to be *gigantic*. It may be said that he found the key in England which has opened the gate for him, and it is often observed that *c'est le premier pas qui coûte* [it's the first step that takes the effort]; but if he did borrow an English key, the lock was so dreadfully rusty, that no common arm would have strength enough to turn it....[14]

Polite letters continued between the two, Champollion asking on 23 November 1822 for the use of Bankes' copy of a hieroglyphic list of kings from a temple of Rameses II at Abydos, now in the British Museum. In this letter he demonstrated his reading of the name of Rameses as found on the king list and also that of Tuthmes. Friendship turned to rivalry following the enthusiastic public reactions to the published *Lettre*. Young died several years later on 10 May 1829. His memorial in Westminster Abbey pointedly records the claim that 'he first penetrated the obscurity which had veiled for ages the hieroglyphics of Egypt', and his letters were published posthumously in 1855 in an attempt to show that he had discovered the 'Egyptian alphabet' 'several years before Champollion suspected its existence'. The preface makes this programmatic intent clear, referring to 'the ingenious but unscrupulous Frenchman'.[15]

The full realization of the nature of the hieroglyphic script, hinted at in Champollion's *Lettre*, was not published until 1824. The *Précis du système hiéroglyphique des anciens égyptiens par M. Champollion le jeune* marks the decisive step in decipherment, and the fame that this brought restored Champollion to political respectability with the French authorities. A later edition, which followed in 1828, included a description of 'determinative' picture-signs (see above p. 21): Champollion had studied the circular zodiac, which had been removed from the Temple of Dendera by a French engineer in 1820–21 and was now displayed in the Louvre, and he showed that some signs were pictures indicating the category of the preceding words. Even if one allows that Champollion was more familiar with Young's initial work than he subsequently claimed, he is the sole decipherer of the hieroglyphic script: any decipherment stands or falls as a whole, and while Young discovered parts of an alphabet – a key – Champollion unlocked an entire written language.

In the spring of 1824 Champollion travelled briefly to England with his brother and visited the British Museum. It was the only time that the decipherer gazed on the Stone itself, as opposed to the copies of the inscription. He then set off for Egypt with a Franco-Tuscan scientific expedition, and by the time he arrived at Wadi Halfa he could write on 1 January 1829 to Dacier that 'our alphabet is good' for all periods of Egyptian history.[16] For the first time in centuries the great monuments that survived throughout the country were legible. His decipherment opened up millennia of human history and resolved the pharaonic chronology that had been a major concern of the period; it also showed that human history went back much further than was accepted in the Church's chronology based on the Bible.

This period also saw the foundation of major Egyptian collections outside Egypt, and on Champollion's return to Paris from Egypt in 1830 he was installed as curator at the Louvre. He died from a stroke on 4 March 1832, probably due in part to exhaustion. He had already completed the sheets of his great *Grammaire égyptien*, which he entrusted to his brother as his 'calling card to posterity'. His death at the relatively early age of forty-one added to the romanticism of his role. His former teacher, de Sacy, spoke the funerary eulogy in the Académie des Inscriptions et Belles Lettres, raising him to mythical status as the decipherer of the Sphinx's riddle, the 'new Oedipus' (a claim that Kircher had made for himself). The scholar John Gardner Wilkinson's (1797–1875) comments, in a letter to another British traveller and antiquarian, Robert Hay (1799–1863), also expressed a sense of deep shock even among the English:

What a loss – there is an end to hieroglyphics – for say what they like no one knew anything about the subject but himself, though wrong – as must necessarily happen in a similar study – in some instances.[17]

Champollion was buried in Père Lachaise cemetery in Paris under a simple obelisk, inscribed only with his name 'Champollion le jeune'; his elder brother supervised the publication of his posthumous papers, but the decipherment remained a speculative hypothesis to many scholars. As late as 1854 the orientalist and archaeologist Gustavus Seyffarth (1796–1885) was still opposing Champollion's work, and lecturing in New York under the highly spurious billing the 'discoverer of the key to the hieroglyphs'.

In Europe the lead in Egyptology quickly passed to Germany through the achievements of Karl Richard Lepsius (1810–84), who learnt from Champollion's posthumous *Grammaire*, accepting, correcting and expanding his system. On an expedition to Egypt in April 1866 Lepsius studied another trilingual inscription found at Tanis on a fine limestone stela, with a copy of the Canopus Decree of Ptolemy III (238 BC), now in the Egyptian Museum, Cairo. With this discovery Champollion's hypothesis could be checked using a hieroglyphic text that had a definitely identified ancient translation, and his decipherment became an uncontestable certainty. From 1822 onwards Egyptology has developed into a truly international arena of collaboration, continuing the spirit in which the first copies of the Rosetta Stone were circulated.

A modern icon of understanding

The Rosetta Stone is among the best-known inscriptions in the world, although, given the sacerdotal nature of its contents, it is now largely read only by specialists. From the moment of its rediscovery the Rosetta Stone has been both a contested object between warring nations and part of world heritage. It has turned from the booty of conflict into a symbol of cross-cultural understanding, and has opened up 3,000 years of written history, revealing a vast amount of hitherto unintelligible world literature and records of human experience and desires that had been thought lost for ever. It has entered the English language as a phrase for 'a key to some previously unattainable understanding' (*Oxford English Dictionary*), and continues to give its name to translation programmes, and even space missions, such as that launched by the European Space Agency in March

2004 to decipher the early history of the solar system, 4,600 million years ago, by investigating the origin and composition of a comet.

The fascination with the Rosetta Stone comes not from its material form but from the concept of its importance in the history of writing; it has featured visually in surprisingly few pieces of visual art or Egyptomania. The grandest reproduction is the commemorative pavement entitled 'Ex-Libris J.-F. Champollion (Figeac)' in the Musée Champollion, Figeac, by Joseph Kossuth in 1991 (fig. 19). The Stone's principal media of visual dissemination, however, are numerous museum souvenirs, including mouse-mats, T-shirts and paperweights, as well as replicas of various sizes. For several decades it has been the top-selling postcard produced by the British Museum. Nevertheless, its significance is so conceptual that many visitors who are fully aware of the Stone's importance are uncertain of its precise size and appearance before visiting the gallery where it is displayed.

The Rosetta Stone is the most popular single artefact in the British Museum's collections, and as such has never been removed from the Museum, except to shelter it from bombing in the World Wars (in 1918 it was moved to a disused tube tunnel). On one other occasion, in October 1972, the Museum's Trustees agreed, after an initial refusal, to let the Stone travel to Paris for the 150th anniversary of the *Lettre à M. Dacier*. It was displayed for a month in the Henri IV gallery at Champollion's own museum, the Louvre. At this time national rivalries about decipherment were still intense enough for complaints about the permanent display to be occasionally received from French visitors to the British Museum saying that Champollion's portrait was smaller than Young's on the accompanying information panels; complaints from English visitors, however, were made that Young's was smaller. Both were actually the same size.

This fascination with the Stone has directly affected its display and its appearance: it was displayed at an angle (fig. 20) and was all too often seen as a black-and-white flat surface, like a piece of printed text. This was due to the

19 The Rosetta Stone as featured in *La place des écritures* in the Musée Champollion, Figeac, by Joseph Kossuth (1991).

white infill and the wax which absorbed dirt from the
London atmosphere over two centuries, obscuring the
Stone's true colour. Much of the dark colour was also due
to a deposit of finger grease from visitors reaching out and
touching it, so much so that from the mid-nineteenth
century it was described as 'black basalt'. In 1999 a small
sample of stone was taken from the underside and analysed,
revealing that it is a fine- to medium-grained quartz-rich
rock containing feldspar, amphibole and mica. Following
this, the Stone was fully conserved to reveal its sparkling
appearance as a grey granodioroite with a pink vein of
granite. This conservation work was done in the gallery
so that the Stone could remain on display to visitors at all
times (fig. 21). The cleaning took three weeks, with a team
under Eric Miller of the British Museum's Department
of Conservation, and used liniment of soap (a mixture
of camphor, oleic acid, rosemary oil, and potassium
hydroxide) and acid-free tissue poultices. These were put
on each evening and left on overnight; the next morning,

21 The Rosetta Stone being cleaned in 1999.

22 *Overleaf* The Rosetta Stone in 2004.

before the Museum opened to the public, the poultices were removed, and the surface was carefully swabbed with liniment of soap, white spirit, acetone and de-ionized water. No ancient pigment or nineteenth-century traces were removed, apart from the modern white infill that had been last retouched in the 1980s.

This work was undertaken to celebrate the bicentenary of the Stone's discovery, with an international exhibition that was held in the Museum, running from 10 July 1999 to 16 January 2000. It was opened by HE Adel el-Gazzar, the ambassador of the Arab Republic of Egypt to Great Britain, who spoke warmly of the international cooperation between Egypt and other nations that has advanced modern Egyptology, and of which the Stone, with its international history, is also a symbol. For the first time since antiquity, the conserved Stone was placed upright on its original base, giving it back its character as an ancient Egyptian temple stela, and not as an abstracted portion of text (fig. 22). It stood on its base perfectly.

4

Egypt

The key to Egyptian hieroglyphs

23 The inscriptions on
the Rosetta Stone.

As the Classicist Mary Beard has remarked, 'The Stone itself, and the decipherment that it allowed, has come to be constructed as a talisman for the museum, for museum culture and for the past time that that culture claims to embody. The Stone acts as an almost mystical key to the hidden world of history.'[18] Through museums this world of history is now international and universally accessible, but our understanding of the past is always as fragmentary as the Stone. The Rosetta Stone itself is so familiar that it can encourage us to assume an over-simplified process of 'reading' another culture, a sort of textual colonialism in which the ancient world is fed into a stony code-breaking machine and is decoded into something familiar and comprehensible. And just as hieroglyphs were once thought to be images of ideas, it is easy to assume that texts are simple reflections of a lost reality. However, ancient texts are never just windows on the past: in ancient Egypt, literacy was very restricted and so all texts are elite products. As such they embody a particular world-view developed by a small percentage of the population, and only describe certain aspects of their world. The Rosetta Stone, with its hierarchy of different scripts and languages, embodies this aspect of written records, as well as being a key to deciphering them. It reminds us that the omissions from texts can only by filled by archaeology and comparative studies. While it is easy to trace the shape of the signs on this stela, it is much harder to trace the movement of the minds and the lives that lie behind them, and that world can only be sensed by reading between the lines. In this way the Rosetta Stone stands as a reminder that the decipherment of the ancient past is a continuous international process that is repeated and reshaped at every reading of a text or artefact; like any act of reading, it is a fragile process of dialogue. And while the Stone has always been, from the moment of its creation, an artefact created by, and contested between, different competing cultures, it is nevertheless also a symbol of their ability to communicate with and decipher each other across space and time. Broken and slightly battered, it remains a symbol of the enduring power of human understanding.

Translation of the Demotic text of the Rosetta Stone

by R.S. Simpson

24 A decorated page from the first translation of the Rosetta Stone in the New Word published by the Philomathean Society, Philadelphia, 1858.

Revised version from R.S. Simpson, *Demotic Grammar in the Ptolemaic Sacerdotal Decrees* (Oxford, 1996), 258–71.

[Year 9, Xandikos day 4], which is equivalent to the Egyptian month, second month of Peret, day 18, of the King 'The Youth who has appeared as King in the place of his Father', the Lord of the Uraei 'Whose might is great, who has established Egypt, causing it to prosper, whose heart is beneficial before the gods', (the One) Who is over his Enemy 'Who has caused the life of the people to prosper, the Lord of the Years of Jubilee like Ptah-Tenen, King like Pre', [the King of the Upper Districts and] the Lower Districts 'The Son of the Father-loving Gods, whom Ptah has chosen, to whom Pre has given victory, the Living Image of Amun', the Son of Pre 'Ptolemy, living forever, beloved of Ptah, the Manifest God whose excellence is fine', son of Ptolemy and Arsinoe, the Father-loving Gods, (and) the Priest of Alexander and the Saviour Gods and [the Brother-and-Sister Gods and the] Beneficent [Gods] and the Father-loving Gods and King Ptolemy, the Manifest God whose excellence is fine, Aetos son of Aetos; while Pyrrha daughter of Philinos was Prize-bearer before Berenice the Beneficent, while Areia daughter of Diogenes was [Basket]-bearer [before Arsi]noe the Brother-loving, and while Eirene daughter of Ptolemy was Priestess of Arsinoe the Father-loving: on this day, a decree of the *mr-šn* priests and the *ḥm-nṯr* priests, and the priests who enter the sanctuary to perform clothing rituals for the gods, and the scribes of the divine book and the scribes of the House of Life, and the other priests who have come from the temples of Egypt [to Memphis on] the festival of the Reception of the Rulership by King Ptolemy, living forever, beloved of Ptah, the Manifest God whose excellence is fine, from his father, who have assembled in the temple of Memphis, and who have said:

Whereas King Ptolemy, living forever, the Manifest God whose excellence is fine, son of King Ptolemy [and Queen] Arsinoe, the Father-loving Gods, is wont to do many favours for the temples of Egypt and for all those who are subject to his kingship, he being a god, the son of a god and a goddess, and being like Horus son of Isis and Osiris, who protects his father Osiris, and his heart being beneficent concerning the gods, since he has given much money and much grain to the temples of Egypt, [he having undertaken great expenses] in order to create peace in Egypt and to establish the temples, and having rewarded all the forces that are subject to his rulership; and of the revenues and taxes that were in force in Egypt he had reduced some or(?) had renounced them completely, in order to cause the army and all the other people to be prosperous in his time as [king; the arrear]s which were due to the King from the people who are in Egypt and all those who are subject to his kingship, and (which) amounted to a large total, he renounced; the people who were in prison and those against whom there had been charges for a long time, he released; he ordered concerning the endowments of the gods, and the money and the grain that are given as allowances to their [temples] each year, and the shares that belong to the gods from the vineyards, the orchards, and all the rest of the property which they possessed under his father, that they should remain in their possession; moreover, he ordered concerning the priests that they should not pay their tax on becoming priests above what they used to pay up to Year 1 under his father; he released the people [who hold] the offices of the temples from the voyage they used to make to the Residence of Alexander each year; he ordered that no rower should be impressed into service; he renouced the two-thirds share of the fine linen that used to be made in the temples for the Treasury, he bringing into its [correct] state everything that had abandoned its (proper) condition for a long time, and taking all care to have done in a correct manner what is customarily done for the gods, likewise causing justice to be done for the people in accordance with what Thoth the Twice-great did; moreover, he ordered concerning those who will return from the fighting men and the rest of the people who had gone astray (*lit.* been on other ways) in the disturbance that had occurred in Egypt that [they] should [be returned] to their homes, and their possessions should be restored to them; and he took all care to send (foot)soldiers, horsemen, and ships against those who came by the shore and by the sea to make an attack on Egypt; he spent a great amount in money and grain against these (enemies), in order to ensure that the temples and the people who were in Egypt should be secure; he went to the fortress of Šk3n [which had] been fortified by the rebels with all kinds of work, there being much gear and all kinds of equipment within it; he enclosed that fortress with a wall and a dyke(?) around (*lit.* outside) it, because of the rebels who were inside it, who had already done much harm to Egypt, and abandoned the way of the commands of the King and the commands [of the god]s; he caused the canals which supplied water to that fortress to be dammed off, although the previous kings could not have done likewise, and much money was expended on them; he assigned a force of footsoldiers and horsemen to the mouths of those canals, in order to watch over them and to protect them, because of the [rising] of the water, which was great in Year 8, while those canals supply water to much land and are very deep; the King took that fortress by storm in a short time; he overcame the rebels who were within it, and slaughtered them in accordance with what Pre and Horus son of Isis did to those who had rebelled against them in those places in the Beginning; (as for) the rebels who had gathered armies and led them to disturb the nomes, harming the temples and abandoning the way of the King and his father, the gods let him overcome them at Memphis during the festival of the Reception of the Rulership which he did from his father, and he had them slain on the wood; he remitted the arrears that were due to the King from the temples up to Year 9, and amounted to a large total of money and grain; likewise the value of the fine linen that was due from the temples from what is made for the Treasury, and the verification fees(?) of what had been made up to that time; moreover, he ordered concerning the artaba of wheat per aroura of land, which used to be collected from the fields of the endowment, and likewise for the wine per aroura of land from the vineyards of the gods' endowments: he renounced them; he did many favours for Apis and Mnevis, and the other sacred animals that are honoured in Egypt, more than what those who were before him used to do, he being devoted to their affairs at all times, and giving what is required for their burials, although it is great and splendid, and providing what is dedicated(?) in their temples when festivals are celebrated and burnt offerings made before them, and the rest of the things which it is fitting to do; the honours which are due to the temples and the other honours of Egypt he caused to be established in their (proper) condition in accordance with the law; he gave much gold, silver, grain, and other items for the Place of Apis; he had it adorned with new work as very fine work; he had new temples, sanctuaries, and altars set up for the gods, and caused others to assume their (proper) condition, he having the heart of a beneficent god concerning the gods and enquiring after the honours of the temples, in order to renew them in his time as king in the manner that is fitting; and the gods have given him in return for these things strength, victory, success(?), prosperity, health, and all the (*sic*) other favours, his kingship being established under him and his descendants forever:

   With good fortune! It has seemed fitting to the priests of all the temples of Egypt, as to the honours which are due to King Ptolemy, living forever, the Manifest God whose excellence is fine, in the temples, and those which are due to the Father-loving Gods, who brought him into being, and those which are due to the Beneficent Gods, who brought into being those who brought him into being, and those which are due to the Brother-and-Sister Gods, who brought into being those who brought them into being, and those which are due to the Saviour Gods, the ancestors of his ancestors, to increase them; and that a statue should be set up for King Ptolemy, living forever, the Manifest God whose excellence is fine – which should be called 'Ptolemy who has protected the Bright Land', the meaning of which is 'Ptolemy who has preserved Egypt' – together with a statue for the local god, giving him a scimitar of victory, in each temple, in the public part of the temple, they being made in the manner of Egyptian work; and the priests should pay service to the statues in each temple three times a day, and they should lay down sacred objects before them and do for them the rest of the things that is normal to do, in accordance with what is done for the other gods on the festivals, the processions, and the named (holi)days; and there should be produced a cult image for King Ptolemy, the Manifest God whose excellence is fine, son of Ptolemy and Queen Arsinoe, the Father-loving Gods, together with the (*sic*) shrine in each temple, and it should be installed in the sanctuary with the other shrines; and when the great festivals occur, on which the gods are taken in procession, the shrine of the Manifest God whose excellence is fine should be taken in procession with them; and in order that the shrine may be recognized, now and in the rest of the times that are to come, ten royal diadems of gold should be added – there being one uraeus on them each, like what is normally done for the gold diadems – on top of the shrine, instead of the uraei that are upon the rest of the shrines; and the double crown should be in the centre of the diadems, because it is the one with which the King was crowned in

the temple of Memphis, when there was being done for him what is
normally done at the Reception of the Rulership; and there should be
placed on the upper side of (the) square(?) which is outside the diadems,
and opposite the gold diadem that is described above, a papyrus plant and
a 'sedge' plant; and a uraeus should be placed on a basket with a 'sedge'
under it on the right of the side on top of the shrine, and a uraeus with
a basket under it should be placed on a papyrus on the left, the meaning
of which is 'The King who has illumined Upper and Lower Egypt'; and
whereas fourth month of Shemu, last day, on which is held the birthday
of the King, has been established already as a procession festival in the
temples, likewise second month of Peret, day 17, on which are performed
for him the ceremonies of the Reception of the Rulership – the beginning
of the good things that have happened to everyone: the birth of the King,
living forever, and his reception of the rulership – let these days, the 17th
and the last, become festivals each month in all the temples of Egypt; and
there should be performed burnt offerings, libations, and the rest of the
things that are normally done on the other festivals, on both festivals each
month; and what is offered in sacrifice(?) should be distributed as a
surplus(?) to the people who serve in the temple; and a procession festival
should be held in the temples and the whole of Egypt for King Ptolemy,
living forever, the Manifest God whose excellence is fine, each year, from
first month of Akhet, day 1, for five days, with garlands being worn, burnt
offerings and libations being performed, and the rest of the things that it is
fitting to do; and the priests who are in each of the temples of Egypt should
be called 'The Priests of the Manifest God whose excellence is fine' in
addition to the other priestly titles, and they should write it on every
document, and they should write the priesthood of the Manifest God
whose excellence is fine on their rings and they should engrave it on them;
and it should be made possible for the private persons also who will (so)
wish, to produce the likeness of the shrine of the Manifest God whose
excellence is fine, which is (discussed) above, and to keep it in their homes
and hold the festivals and the processions which are described above, each
year, so that it may become known that the inhabitants of Egypt pay
honour to the Manifest God whose excellence is fine in accordance with
what is normally done; and the decree should be written on a stela of hard
stone, in sacred writing, document writing, and Greek writing, and it
should be set up in the first-class temples, the second-class temples and
the third-class temples, next to the statue of the King, living forever.

Notes

1 M. Coe, *Breaking the Maya Code* (New York, 1992), 37.
2 'The Glory of the Ptolemies' (1911); see C. Cavafy, *Poèmes* (trans. M. Yourcenar and C. Dimara; Paris, 1978), 101.
3 E.M. Forster, *Pharos and Pharillon* (London, 1983 [1923]), 31.
4 D.W. Young, 'A Monastic Invective against Egyptian Hieroglyphs' in D.W. Young, *Studies Presented to Hans Jakob Polotsky* (Beacon Hill, Massachusetts, 1981), 348–60 (quotation from 354).
5 Quoted in O. el-Daly, 'Ancient Egypt in Medieval Arabic Writings' in P. Ucko and T. Champion (eds), *The Wisdom of Egypt: Changing Visions Through the Ages* (Encounters with Ancient Egypt, London, 2003), 39–63 (quotation from 48).
6 T.H. Turner in *Archaeologia: or Miscellaneous Tracts relating to Antiquity* (The Society of Antiquaries of London) 16 (1812), 212–14 (quotation from 214).
7 A letter of Thomas Young to William Bankes' father (10 February 1818): R. Parkinson, *Cracking Codes: The Rosetta Stone and Decipherment* (London, 1999), 32.
8 X.-B. Saintine et al., *Histoire scientifique et militaire de l'éxpedition française en Égypte* (Paris, 1832) VI, 434–5; quoted:

C. Lagier, *Autour de la pierre de Rosette* (Brussels, 1927), 8–9.
9 Letter of 6 September 1801, quoted in R. Solé and D. Valbelle (trans. S. Rendall), *The Rosetta Stone: The Story of the Decoding of Hieroglyphics* (London, 2001), 33.
10 E.D. Clarke, *Travels in Various Countries of Europe, Asia and Africa* II.2 *Greece, Egypt and the Holy Land* (London, 1814), 273.
11 *Archaeologia: or Miscellaneous Tracts relating to Antiquity* (The Society of Antiquaries of London) 16 (1812), 212–14 (quotation from 213).
12 *The Gentleman's Magazine* 72 (1802), 726–7.
13 *Supplement to the Encyclopaedia Britannica* IV. 1 (1819), 35.
14 J. Leitch (ed.), *Miscellaneous Works of the Late Thomas Young* (London, 1855), 220.
15 J. Leitch (ed.), *Miscellaneous Works of the Late Thomas Young* (London, 1855), iv–vi.
16 J.-F. Champollion (ed. H. Hartleben), *Lettres et journaux écrits pendant le voyage d'Égypte* (Paris, 1986), 181.
17 Quoted in J. Thompson, *Sir Gardner Wilkinson and his Circle* (Austin, 1992), 126–7.
18 M. Beard, 'Souvenirs of Culture: Deciphering (in) the Museum' in *Art History* 15.4 (1992), 505–32 (quotation from 521).

Further reading

Adkins, L. and R., *The Keys to Egypt: The Race to Read the Hieroglyphs* (London, HarperCollins, 2000) [a biography of Champollion].

Andrews, C. and Quirke, S., *The Rosetta Stone: Facsimile Drawing* (London, British Museum Publications, 1988) [official publication; out of print].

Baines, J., Huston, S. and Cooper, J., 'Last writing: script obsolescence in Egypt, Mesopotamia and Mesoamerica' in *Comparative Studies in Society and History* 45 (2003), 430–79.

Beard, M., 'Souvenirs of culture: deciphering (in) the Museum' in *Art History* 15.4 (1992), 505–32 [a description and analysis of previous displays].

Bierbrier, M., 'The acquisition by the British Museum of antiquities discovered during the French invasion of Egypt' in W.V. Davies (ed.), *Studies in Egyptian Antiquities: A Tribute to T.G.H. James* (British Museum Occasional Paper 123, London, British Museum, 1999), 111–13.

Coleman, S. and Elsner, J., 'Epilogue: landscapes reviewed' in id. (eds), *Pilgrimage Past and Present: Sacred Travel and Sacred Space in the World Religions* (London, British Museum Press, 1995), 196–220 [on the Stone's role in perceptions of the British Museum].

Collier, M. and Manley, B., *How to Read Egyptian Hieroglyphs* (London, British Museum Press, 1998) [an introduction to hieroglyphs].

Cruz-Uribe, E., 'The Death of Demotic at Philae: A Study in Pilgrimage and Politics' in T.A. Bács (ed.), *A Tribute to Excellence: Studies Offered in Honor of Ernö Gaál, Ulrich Luft, László Török*, 163–84. *Studia Aegyptiaca 17* (Budapest, 2002), 163–84.

el-Daly, O., *Egyptology, the Missing Millennium: Ancient Egypt in Medieval Muslim Arabic Writings* (London, University College Press, 2003).

Derchain, P., *Le dernier obélisque* (Brussels, Fondation égyptologique Reine Élisabeth, 1987) [the history of Hadrian's obelisk].

Devauchelle, D., *La Pierre de Rosette* (Musée Champollion, Figeac, Editions Alternatives, 2003).

Laissus, Y., *L'Égypte, une aventure savante: Avec Bonaparte, Kléber, Menou 1798–1801* (Paris, Fayard, 1998).

Leclant, J., 'Le voyage de Jean-Nicolas Huyot en Égypte (1818–1819) et les manuscrits de Nestor l'Hôte' in *Bulletin de la Société Française d'Egyptologie* 32 (1961), 35–42.

Leclère, F., *Les villes de basse Egypte au Ier millénaire av. J.C.: Analyse archéologique et historique de la topographie urbaine* (DPhil. Université de Lille III, 1997), 102–26 [on Sais].

McDowell, A., *Village Life in
Ancient Egypt: Laundry Lists
and Love Songs* (Oxford, Oxford
University Press, 1999)
[an anthology of texts from
an ancient village].
Middleton, A. and Klemm, D.,
'The geology of the Rosetta
Stone' in *Journal of Egyptian
Archaeology* 89 (2003), 207–16.
Parkinson, R., *Cracking Codes:
The Rosetta Stone and
Decipherment* (London, British
Museum Press and Berkeley,
University of California Press,
1999) [exhibition catalogue].
Parkinson, R., *Pocket Guide to
Egyptian Hieroglyphs* (London,
British Museum Press and New
York, Barnes and Noble, 2003)
[an introduction to the
hieroglyphic script].
Simpson, W.K. (ed.), *The Literature
of Ancient Egypt: An Anthology
of Stories, Instructions, Stelae,
Autobiographies and Poetry*
(New Haven and London,
Yale University Press, 2003).
Reid, D.M., *Whose Pharaohs?
Archaeology, Museums, and
Egyptian National Identity
from Napoleon to World War I*
(Berkeley, Los Angeles and
London, University of
California Press, 2002).
Solé, R. and Valbelle, D. (trans.
S. Rendall), *The Rosetta Stone:
The Story of the Decoding of
Hieroglyphics* [sic] (London,
Profile Books, 2001).
Usick, P., *Adventures in Egypt and
Nubia: The Travels of William
John Bankes* (1786–1855)

(London, British Museum
Press, 2002).
Valbelle, D. and Leclant J., *Le décret
de Memphis: Colloque de la
Fondation Singer-Polignac à
l'occasion de la célébration du
bicentenaire de la découverte
de la Pierre de Rosette* (Paris,
De Boccard, 1999).
Wilson, P. 2001–,
http://www.dur.ac.uk/penelope.
wilson/sais.html [website on
the expedition to Sais].

Photographic credits

1 British Museum, EA 24
2 British Museum
3 Egyptian Museum, Cairo,
  CG 22816
4 Dr Penny Wilson
5 Richard Parkinson
6 British Library
7 Richard Parkinson
8 Richard Parkinson
9 British Museum
10 Dr M.L. Bierbrier
11 British Museum
12 *Illustrated London News*
13 Collection Maison Champollion,
   musée départemental
14 By kind permission of
   Mr and Mrs S.Z. Young
15 British Museum
16 Courtesy of the National
   Trust Photographic Library/
   Richard Pink
17 Bankes papers XI.A.108;
   courtesy of the National Trust
18 British Museum
19 'Ex-Libris J.-F. Champollion
   (Figeac)', Joseph Kosuth, 1991,
   photograph Nelly Blaya
20 British Museum
21 British Museum
22 British Museum
23 British Museum
24 Philomathean Society of the
   University of Pennsylvania,
   Philadelphia